SHADOWS
OF A
VAGABOND

CHAMPION PRESS, LTD.

BEVERLY HILLS

CHAMPION PRESS, LTD.
BEVERLY HILLS, CALIFORNIA

Grateful acknowledgment is given to the following publications in which certain poems have
appeared: INTERIM, PERCEPTIONS, MISNOMER, AFTERWORK, EGORAG,
ANACONDA, MOBIUS, DEVIANCE, POETRY JOURNAL and BROKEN STREETS.

Back cover photograph by Mary S. Toth of Portraits Today, Port Washington, Wisconsin
Designed by Pilot Publishing, Milwaukee, Wisconsin

Library of Congress Catalog Card Number 97-76842

Cataloging-in-Publication Data
Noel, Brook.
Shadows of a vagabond: a collection of poetry / by Brook Noel. —1st ed.
p. cm.
Preassigned LCCN: 97-76842
ISBN: 1-891400-06-1
1. Love poetry. 2. Interpersonal relations—Poetry. 3. Loss (Psychology)—Poetry. I. Title.
PS3564.O45S43 1998   811'.54
QB197-41292

Manufactured in the United States of America

10 9 8 7 6 5 4 3 2 1

for my silent vagabond

Table of Contents

I
THE GLIMMER

II
THE GAME

III
THE GIMMICK

IV
THE GOLD

V
THE GRIEF

VI
THE GOOD BYE

SHADOWS
OF A
VAGABOND

a collection of poetry by

Brook Noel

I

THE GLIMMER

Evasive Man

I haven't been able
to find words for you yet.
Everything I've ever known,
I've pinned down, stalked it,
until its melted and dripped
from this pen.

But you elude me.
I kiss the bottom of a beer bottle,
stare at the blue letters on a Triscuit box,
I run away and hibernate for a weekend
wondering if the words are in the forest -
maybe below this crusted layer of ice.

I would like to dive for them
or for you - or fish chips - anything
if it would release me, release you.
Give me my poem.

Cartwheels On The Moon

I look up
to see you dancing
cartwheels on the moon

eyes howling

and this is not how I thought it would be

as the sun rises and sets
god manipulating puppet strings
up and down
down and up

you do cartwheels on the moon

unsure of gravity or law
or the past that says
we are not who we claim to be

but I join you anyway
doing cartwheels on the moon

Standing

The one standing with the blue velvet eyes
staring at me
inside this crystal ball I live in
you touched me
and now yearn for it again
I told you once, velcro is addictive
and still a sin.

If I brush your shoulder
would you return my stare?
You're so cool, so tough,
so everything,
why don't you dare me
to trap you
inside a moonlit night
where we can fly paper airplanes
and maybe see how gravity turns.
If we can't defy it
perhaps we will learn
what to do when we fall.

Too fast.
Too soon.
Too hard.

Mindless

I am standing in this void of colorless minds —
        — wrapping these vines
around my soul.

Wondering what you would do
        if I crossed that line
        if I chose not to swim back
        if I chose to jump
        if I chose
                to dream inside your mind.
                and twirl my dances down your throat.

I have always been a dancer.

I can cry at night
as can you
and our tears
can create
this lostness.
It's almost 3D.
                Dance with me.

I Will Not Run

We stand.
I see my soul in your eyes
      and I reach for it.

I have waited for this forever.
I have wanted you forever.

We touch.
      And it feels like home.

We ride through each other like a merry-go-round
      slow then fast, we cannot stop or slow
                    down
      and I don't want to.

I am drowning in this pleasure.
The death I've always wanted.

I look up
      and see candy in your eyes
      and it feels like home.

            I am home.

Evasive Man II

I see you in the weirdest places:
under that coaster with the maroon insignia;
inside the hollow curve of the letter P;
clinging to the last piece of scotch tape.

You are that space between the comma
and the L, and I feel a bit like punctuation
trying to find you. My red pen in hand,
scared to cross you out. Sometimes,
the spelling does not matter.

I take this cocoon, worn for too many winters,
and shed it for you, layer by layer.
I will emerge when this clock strikes ten.
(I know it's supposed to be midnight
but I can't make it that long without you.)
That is not a weakness.
Just give me my answer.

And I am dancing again.
It's all I seem to do anymore.
Twirling through these rooms of my mind-
for the ghost, or the demons, or your heart,
I can't really tell the difference.
Moving for a rhythm to sustain this pulse.
Wishing you were here.
I know you would smile,

then lay down and beg me to come closer.
And I would.
That is how it happens in my mind—
every time.

I made your name my password
because I think it has always been
some sort of key. Or at least it feels like one
these nights we twist and shed our veils.
Mine has always been black and torn,
as is yours, but neither of us care.
You are too busy listening to my poems.
And I like that.

You will only want what you cannot have.
I have seen this since the beginning
and moved towards you anyway.
I remind you, that is my fault.
I knew full well.

But for now, you sit on your rock
and I sit on mine. And this is not a glacier,
nor an iceberg. I count the miles on my map
and think about walking. But I know

sooner or later
the stars will have their way with us.
It's out of our control now.
As I dance around the axis of your mind,
I believe it always has been.

II
THE GAME

Holding On

The only thing holding us back
    is our hearts
      and minds
all sheltered within us

The only thing that is not feeling
    is that which
      feels
    intensely.

I could spend my life running
    and I may

searching for an undiscovered island
    to mount my black and blue flag

    but you remain the ocean

I'll have to swim through

I Gave It Away

I take these words you gave me —
bulging with hidden meaning and
too many vowels — and syllable by syllable
I give them to this man lying next to me.
He asked for them, and you weren't here.
I needed no other reason to lead him
head to toe, through your language.

Words like summer's breath, violets,
or comets, leaving a trail on my flesh.
It was the only way to betray you
and it felt like heaven.
And I'm still not sorry for it.

I thought of you though,
staring at the phone,
encased in some black night.
You could have been here. You chose not.
And I made my own choice, finally.

But I have never been a good liar.
This man next to me, his hands drifting,
I, feeling like a Chinese finger trap,
and I sigh, pretending I like it,
because I want to.

Shortly, he will turn to me
and say it was the best ever.
And I will nod, noncommittally.
He will sigh, the pant of a husky dog
that has run too far for his master.

And I know it's quite past two
but that's okay.
Tonight, I gave the words away.
Tomorrow, will never come.

The UFO In Titletown

It was you who left this pit here,
black and empty, like a child
screaming for food.
I had nothing to do with it.
You have always said that was a copout,
and you can say that now,
but it won't effect me, still.

I had no other choice but to fill it.
You who sits there in some night
waiting for the phone to ring.
This time I didn't dial,
pride thick and heavy like
knotted fingers or gnarls of wood.
This has never been pretty.

The void was gone.
For thirty-seven minutes
I could not remember your name.
Call it diversion, digression, division,
I don't care.
Tonight on a little road called Newton,
someone leaned over and said
that I would be famous.

And in that dark town,
where the UFO crashed,
blinking lights and red trucks,
In that town where silence said
everything
I was freed.

And it tasted
like salt
and beer
and grace.

Standing Inside Gray Haze

You cannot tell me life is so black and white
    that you never saw me standing here
        naked in the gray haze

That would be a lie

You cannot tell me that you never wondered
      what it might be like to touch me.
    That would be more of a sin
      than me lying naked on this cross

And like a prophet you speak to me in a dream

in a dream
where I touch you
and you wake up
sweating

Mr.

I would give all my balloons
if when I returned
you were dreaming on my pillow.
I know it is a fantasy
but my head is filled with chestnuts
and I need you to shuck me.

A Poem For You

I am living in this hollow space
between your eyes and mine, straining
to see through to that green side. Straining
to see something other than the stone monument
of our kiss, that never was.

I try day and night
to record you in words. Before you chip,
a cheap vase from a rummage sale that
promised beauty. It lied to me.

I'd like to record your eyes, that smirk,
but I can't see them anymore. Not clear
enough to breathe words into your lungs.
I hate this haze, this frost that covers my body
making me shiver when I remember your face.
The face, I couldn't have, couldn't love,
                          couldn't touch
because you thought it best that way.

I hated your philosophy,
but I loved the man behind it.
Or I thought, but I can't remember
                  the good moments

the ones where we said, *let's not lose this*.
I hate the silence.
This was supposed to be a love poem.
But we never had that.
I gave it to you again and again,
you threw it back
an unwanted fish with no eyes.
But I still kept moving, looking,
eyes rolling down the sidewalk,
like lost pennies.

I know someone will pick this up, someone
will blow on my face and make a wish
and I might be their answer.
Never forgetting that I thought you were mine.

This will fade away, this yearning,
day by day, it will strip from me. Or
I will burn it off, singe it, anything to
make the melting stop.

continued

You have a line, and you will not let me cross it,
by kayak, or dream, or palmistry
but I keep dancing on it anyway, not caring
where I land. I forget tomorrow exists
until I wake up sweating. A horrid dream.

That dream where you make me go away,
shoving these thoughts in a closet, between
yellow towels. Washing my head out with soap.
Watching me dissolve. And in that dream,
I still see you, sitting in that chair and smiling.

This was supposed to be a love poem.

The Seed Pod Exercise

I

I did not choose you
little black thing
you chose me.
She is telling me
to focus on the external.
Okay,
I'll try that.

I spin you through my pointer and thumb
and though you are sharp - you are curved,
not strong enough to cut me.

I wonder what your name is - perhaps
bloated mushroom, frog's toe, or a
fossilized flower that could not grow.

The woman across the room
is staring at you too
I wonder what she sees.
I look at you and see a face
that I would stand on if I could
I have never been that tall.

You are brown and gray and green.
You are the colors of Wisconsin spring
stuck in a blender. Your top looks like
the chocolates my mother once
pressed into sugar cookies.
But you are not that sweet.
I do not need to kiss you to know this.

Your perfect symmetry is your greatest lie.
Lines running through you
division of segments.
I think you tried to do that to me once,
I did not let you.

When I scrape my nail against you
it sounds hollow.
If I squeeze you hard enough you might crumble.
Perhaps, to flip you in my mouth and chew
through you would be best.

I could crush you, kill you, with this grip.
I do.
And if feels a bit
like freedom.

II

My father would never crumble like this
or perhaps he already did.
I was never around to see this, nor was he.
The symmetry of time is a dance of its own.

The hollowness is the same though
as we break apart
there are specs of chewed parsley,
rotting broccoli or something
more viscous.

the parts he hid
the parts i hid too

We are both green like this,
black and bruised. And you
would like to tell me
that is all my fault.
But I slayed those demons long ago
I have enough to carry
on my own.

One part of this earth
that is broken in my hand,
is like a flower.
Circular and even,
trying to hold onto its roots.

I flick it off with my thumbnail.
There were no other words left
yet four minutes to this exercise.
I had no other choice.

I think that piece was her,
beautiful and perfect,
the piece you repel
I fear you are like this dusty, black shell.
I keep squeezing it, crushing it, and
it gets smaller and smaller
but won't disintegrate.

Perhaps if I walked on it with my shoe?
After all,
isn't that what you've always done to me
and I've always done to you?

Paper Moons

If I could squeeze through these wires, I would.
I did not choose this paper box for a house
something from an Origami class,
I don't remember the proper name.

You take a step forward,
walking where I cannot go.
I sit on a pew or a broken piñata
my hands cupped — in prayer — to anything —
looking for a reason to feel like this.

It's a lostness, a loveliness, a hell,
a budding moon that promises nothing more.
But I remain, twirling through night's reflection
Sometimes that's all we have.

The Last Warning

We are looking at each other
a pause inside a madness.
And I can tell you that
I have always yearned like this,
been like this, needed like this,
I never hid it from you.
And now you do cartwheels inside my stomach,
looking for a place to call home.

This is a crusted place
and it knows no light.
I keep my head in the sand most days
just to feel connected to this earth.
I shake when I write
I tremble when I stand
and if you choose to love me
I might disintegrate in your hands.

The Drifter

I have tried
but I am
not a lighthouse
no safety
no island

You throw me
a life vest
with holes

Together
we hunt
through these
bleak winters

longing for our
soul to appear -
a last sunset

III

THE GIMMICK

Together

I remember you
from a distant place

where we drove with the top down
listening to Joplin, dew on our hair

I thought you would never come back

You wonder what happened to the brown cafe
you wonder what happened to my dreams
you wonder what happened to me

And I don't want to talk about it
Let's tie ourselves together

let's not die

The Man In My Closet

There is a black headless man
standing in my closet. We both
know the phone is ringing, but
neither of us move.

One of us must die. That has
long been the truth we deny.

I have been outside,
hoping this is the last snow.
A splinter in my foot.
You put a white dash
on a chalkboard. You
have scored your first point.

Someone is dying again.
Can you hear that echo?
Can you hear her cry?
Hanging on the philosophy
you left her in your will.

Trying to decode your mind, your words
that you spat through the keyhole.
She is trying to reach you again, but
you are not there. You have never been.

Yesterday, I sewed a mast.
For the tugboat in my bathtub.
I sat naked in the water
watching it swirl around,
watching it twirl down the drain,
my skin shriveling beneath the surface.
I couldn't help but smile.

You hold the words under water,
knowing I will put my head under.
Knowing I will drown.

The Garage

I've been sitting in the garage a lot more lately.
Dead center on the cement.
There are only ninety-seven
bottles of beer on this wall.
I count again.
It's still the same.
And I hate the way
it doesn't change.

You tell me that story again
about the woman who put her head in the oven.
You think it's funny.
You wonder why I don't laugh.

Shhh.. I'm counting

to what, I don't know. Infinity
seems like a good hobby
though you have always
preferred stamp collecting.
But they don't put poets on stamps.
Not this year anyway.

So I stay here.

It's a hibernation of sorts.
Pushing the button that makes the door
open and close - open and close.

Whose god Is This?

I smile, and you
record the date on the calendar
I tell you that is blasphemous
you remind me that
I've never been your god.

My body feels like wood most days
I watch you hold the knife, between palms
glazed with sweat, or blood, or tears.
I watch you whittle out the shallow of my neck
I know it's not too late to turn around
or burn myself, but you take pride
in this pile of ashes.
You remind me that I am your creation.
I remind you that you have never been
my god, either.

This is the gold and rust of August's twilight
you look up and tell me
the comet is coming.
We watch it all these clear nights, wondering
what it would say if it might speak.
I think it has come to take me from this place.
That has always been my dream, never yours.

You says it's like Goliath's white tooth,
disintegrating against a black night.
You tell me that I look like
a cavity with a black heart.
I used to love the stars, but you skew them,
connecting them into a shape
that will worship you.
I never will.

You pull the knife out again, whittling away
the muscle in my arm. Carving out my lung.
Taking away my words.

Growing Up

You stand erect, your own king
I will not bow down
I will not limbo inside your reality

my heart skips a beat
and you catch it,
twisting it dry and lifeless
while I blow bubbles through my windpipes

wondering how it came to this

a foreign scent of Wisconsin
radiates off your tongue

I do not believe in fusion
I do not believe in us

the adult realities flooded our sandbox
until it all spilled over
and everything we ever had
seeped into the ground

Between Star Wishes

There are days
I could walk away - never look back
                                    and never cry.
There are ways
to strip you bare of your
sharp hush, scraping my body
   every time it gets too close.

And there are nights
I know - I'd be better off without you

if I could just say good bye.

Stuck between stars, searching for a wish,
trapped inside a dream, I dreamt
                        that came true
"Steamroller," was the word she used
   to describe the love of you.
Walking a plank
would be best now
immersed in blind, wet emotion

swimming towards the freedom
I see dangling off your finger.

This Place

It is in this place
I could fade away
forget my own name.

You wrote it on the wall again.
black letters, bulging at the bottom.

I don't recognize the woman in the mirror.
Spitting at the silver reflection.
A worm in her throat.

I think I used to be someone.
I think I used to feel something.
I think I used to love some man.

There is a tornado in the cabinet.
I won't open that door.
The spinning, a metronome,
of the way it should have been.

I think I used to be someone.

Dry Gin

You stare at the dry gin
making wet circles on the bar.
The transparency is confusing,
and always will be.
I stare at that scar, above your third eye
and you cover it with your hand
but I still see
I always have.

The smirk, with too many teeth
is stuck in my head.
Now, it lands on this paper.
You tell me my skin is beautiful,
and you would like to touch it.
I hold out a callused palm.
You think my lifeline is shrinking
and I don't disagree.

We both know where this is going,
so we don't discuss it.
We stare at the clock, waiting,

for closing time.

Self-Discovery

I

You came here seeking truth,
a dwarf with no head.
Putting your brain in the sand
because there wasn't a better idea.

In that dirt, from that earth
the answers seeped forward,
in through your ears
clinging to your nerves.
Static of fusion.
Call it whatever you like,
it is no less true.

II

And then you hide again, seeking a shell,
not much unlike a hermit crab.
But you don't fit into a beer bottle,
or a smoke — not the way you'd like to anyway.

So instead you ingest them
attempting to swallow your answer
(you can't think of a better place for it
  than the pit of your stomach)
Dying to erase the answer you sought.
It was easier the other way.

And you unscrew your head
tucking it under the bed. Praying
the hotel doesn't have your address.
You will pay cash.
You don't want them to send it back

a postcard will do just fine.

III

At home again, an amnesia of sorts.
You pour yourself a coffee & Kalua
unsure if you want to awake or sleep
but knowing you don't want to be
where you are. But that is all there is.
That is all there ever was.

IV

A day later a letter arrives
with a neat maroon insignia.
You remember writing it,
your best penmanship at 2:00 am
on the night when you questioned
Cupid's inventor.

It reads of everything you remembered
everything you know.

You wrote it down because you knew
you would play this game. Amnesia girl.

The tip of your cigarette taps ashes on
the already yellowed paper.

You don't really care and
that's half the problem.
Lunacy you say,
though you know it's truth
and that has always made you run—
your head tucked under one arm,
knowing one day you will have to emerge.

You pull out your planner.
Not today, you decide, while staring
at a grocery store flyer.
Beer is on sale. That and ham.
Winter is coming — time to stock up.

The Storyteller

I have been creating this story
since the first scene.
You enter: plain, white, Midwestern
but that isn't enough

From the wardrobe of my mind
(outdated)
I dress you: so you will love me
never seeing you for what you are,
or were, before I made you.

and I am paying for that now.
Year seven: I turn into an iguana at
midnight. Who wrote this chapter?

The story needs to end,
closure (that's the trendy term)
but we both hold on, two chapters
before the climax.
Trying to turn back the pages

ignoring the paper
yellowing - disintegrating
beneath our fingers

You ask if this is a trilogy
No. Not even a book two
You scrounge for a bookmark,
wad of gum, anything,
to hold this place — this space —

And I watch you, beg you
to let the cover fall shut
(you know I'm not strong enough)
to close the book. Before the story loses
all its magic, all its words.

Worn / Torn

I think you expect me
to deserve your love
I have a heart
I am deserving enough
I will not fall to my knees
no man is worth
a torn hole in my jeans

IV

THE
GOLD

A Single Moment

Bound by this desire-saturated stare
I move closer - skin on skin
as if we were always meant to be one.

The softest palms dance across my soul.
The deepest eyes stare through my life.
A moment alive, like no other.
The moment that we lived for
arriving beneath a starless sky.

Our mouths unwrap each other
gifts of night, and time, and a closeness
that knows no words.
A moment we should stop and hold.
A moment I would give my life to savor.
A moment suspended out of reality and reason.
A moment that knows no bounds.

continued

You lay me down on a satin world
feeding me dreams one by one
below a silver moon
that promises nothing more
than now.

For once,
that is enough.

Hands of Crimson

Crimson fingertips trace my ribs, before,
when you thought I new, budding,
some promise to redeem your crusted sins.
A plaid tongue burns my breast
stalking rebirth or escape or a heroine
that I have no access to.
A mirror of velvet,
I seek the same on your flesh.
Knowing the trail between your naval and
darkness leads only to the jaded woman
I swore I'd never become.

Words you gave me dissolve in Wisconsin air
most unrecalled, the others justified by
the Santa Ana winds that
make us all talk crazy.
I cut out the letters, paste them to a page,
so I will not forget the pastels you painted.

Tracing Kodak paper with my tongue
to find the pieces you deny, ignoring
how sweet you taste.

Links

I wear your mask to escape my own,
a desert moon pleads for nothing more
than the dew of lovers who've yet to touch
bound by shadows they won't ignore.

You eat summer words from my palm.
In the moment of our first touch
reality becomes just another siren
that neither of us hear.

Legs link us as chains, mouths utter
hollow wishes we call truth, or love,
as torsos shackled together
thrash against the desert's dawn.

Under her harsh light,
we whimper against wet skin
these promises slip between us, coat our flesh,
the only souvenirs we will take home.

You Created Destiny

You say we have so much to talk about
now I find I'm talking to myself
swaying in the silence of the branches-
   Their frost leaves:
   Their sustained hopes:
(maybe you were the one)
but I can't hear you now.
     Have you walked this tundra?
     Turning through the leaves,
     they were promises too.
I have replayed this moment in my head
this moment where
 you say you love me
 you say you'll never leave me
 you say you have waited for me
     I walk alone
     an unfilled destiny
     some lake reflecting my sorrow
and I don't know why I'm here

V

THE
GRIEF

Tomorrow

Tomorrow won't be you
Perhaps the same pain
inflicted by your salt licking
                    tongue
   cut through me
   (your eyes did)
I had a knife that sharp once
and Mother took it away from me
I need her now.
Where is she?
Tomorrow is here
and I am your pain
you are this stain
and again
I see you in every mirror
(shadows may be closer
  than they appear)
A mirage
A lie
you are not here
I am not there
but I will always wear you

as a scar

When We Died

I never meant to kill you, but
you left me no other choice.
(This is a metaphor, of course.)
Or so you hope. As do I. But
spirits die, and you wouldn't breathe
how I needed it, craved it, loved it.

This is hollow. It has always been
carved out. Pumpkin guts and seeds -
between my legs - between my toes.
Kind of like a garden, but so black.
It's like death too.
(A metaphor, of course.)

Leaving so soon, I ask?
I knew you would.

There are no skeletons we haven't resurrected.
A museum of our could've beens
that we never wanted to begin with.
We charge admission
after all we need something
good to come of the wasted time.

Resurrect this wasteland then.
People staring through the glass,
pointing their fingers.
Look at that, they say.
Look at that.

Backwash

It was a gap in the colander
I sifted through
into the drain
filled with pieces of meat
that sifted through your teeth
to feed me.

You called it revenge,
for all those hearts,
that did the same
to you.

Rebirth

Reborn is he
after the seventh beer
only then are his hands recalled,
current, tides, winds and breath -
my flesh the mast he paints on.

Clawing to inhale his scent,
his sweat, my perfume
long faded on cold flesh
that dared not seek again.

Only then might I dissolve
red fingertips on gray keys
praying for the resurrection offered
by his voice.
Fumbling with my own hands
sweaty palms against hot thighs
pushing to forget his absence
hips thrashing to forget his love.

The Shadow

My shadow never loved you.
It was I who was weak,
begging you to cover me
and make the melting stop.

I saw her blackness,
her leopard dress and silver shoes.
I heard her whisper through rusted veins
suicidal promises rest on his tongue.
I devoured you anyway, forgetting
that love cannot withhold death.

Flesh fusing beneath desert air,
reality could be denied.
To live one second cocooned within you
was better than another second spent
watching myself die.

You're only stealing from yourself,
my shadow says. A feather boa
around her neck as she dances.
She will look away. Grant me pardon.
She knows I am not strong enough to stop.

Wait, she hums, *just wait.*

Fourteen days can starve a soul,
dissolve cobalt dreams into hypotheticals
we hang in our closet
terrified to give the remnants away.

I listen to your selective memory
forget all the moments I cling too.
All the moments where night lost its fear,
and your words were true
and I was enough.

Love's Void

Standing on the abyss,
you brush my cheek, saying
that this is all my fault.
I want to choke you, strangle you,
make you die my death.
I want to shatter this shield around you
I want to make you beg.
I long to make you real.

I will not jump, perhaps
I'll push you over. You have long
been on the edge, holding onto my neck
for balance. Choking in your grip,
you tell me this is love.
I feel it slide down my throat,
a poison that erodes but does not kill.

You suggest dinner, a vacation, a hell
for us to paint as heaven.
You have a collection of brushes
and heard that I was an artist.
You tell me just to repaint the world.
You say you heard I like a challenge.
You hand me a brush and a canvas
to darken a night you already stole.

A Lava Death

In 36 hours I went to hell and back.
and I met you there, tar on your face
lava in my teeth and it was a beautiful story.
What did you see when I pulled the rip cord?
When I jumped? When you watched me die,
the second death. Did it feel like home?

For me, it wasn't so bad. Not like the time
you chewed through my flesh with words.
This felt like a future or a beginning.
You always ask how many times
I will die for you.
I am counting on my toes. So many deaths,
and not one of them has brought me life.
Not the way they're supposed to.
Not the way they do in books.

It's this fear of living that makes me die
and each time I shed, this darkness gets thicker.
I saw his eyes on the lava road, and I loved them.
I loved them more than yours.
This reality is suspended,
a dance that knows no floor,
no partner, no rhythm.
I wait for the resurection.

Please borrow me a breath
or a gasp to glorify this story.
I need a touch or a toothbrush
to scrub off the rotted words.

Give me the final word
let's jump together
let's find closure.

Thinking of You

We stand using each other for mirrors
I think you're a dream. You think I'm an angel.
We think in terms of illusions,
creating in each other
what we lost for ourselves.
I skunk you in cribbage
I do not look in your eyes
I do not want to know the price I'll pay.

Every fairy tale can be unraveled
left are nouns and verbs
We can rebuild a horror story.
I know. You know. We will.
We choose not to think of that now.
You feed me words carefully selected
I chew through them like a starving child
You chew through me.

I am trembling when you touch me.
You rub my shoulders until I melt.
We breathe together, gasp together.
For a moment, I would die for you—
everything passes.

Whatever the sunrise brings to our fate
I will remember this, I will hold it
as long as I need to
(I fear forever)
You can forget me.
(we both know you will)

And you have forgotten now
all the things you said.
I wrote them down in a notebook
you hand every piece of me back
I put the remains in my junk drawer.

Forever

We had no initials engraved in moonlight
just a moment we both held.
A moment where we created a forever
that you would close the gate to.

Now I scrub at the rust
falling through the could've beens -
the times I ran through fields
calling to the wind.
If you had stayed — what then?

I have felt your nothingness
and I have felt your thoroughness
and I have heard your teachings
and I have thanked you for this.

But forever drifts through
this dementia caked over our eyes.
And I watch as you make something out
of nothing
and I beg as you make nothing out of
something.

I begged for you to turn around,
to touch my face,
to make it real.

That night you whispered
We'll always find a way,
the words were a soft promised whisper.
I never reminded you of them.
I did not believe you would lie.

But limbs bend,
shadows like the bodies of us,
beneath one sliver of sun meshed in sin.
To cleanse was to wash these tainted souls
with sweat, with anticipation,
with an indigo night
that we called love.

Dawn meant you'd run for that greener place
ignoring this truth.
I watched you run back
to the world we ran from,
a space left under the stars
that only I saw.

VI

THE
GOOD BYE

Go, If You Must

Go into your darkness then,
build yourself a bamboo dream,
or a teepee, or a house connected by shackles.
I won't dare knock. I never asked you to enter.
I never asked you to leave.

You live on your own tightrope,
suspended by stars. You expect me
to dance or hold the net when you fall.
I have never been that strong.
I have never wanted to be.

Horses emerge from your twilight mind
galloping toward me, a mini explosion
and the earth reforms. I count the planets,
you are gone now, there is one less.

Coffee Table

My finger traces the stain on the table
where the heat from your mug
seeped through the lace doily
to leave a beige stain on glass.
It was all you left me
to remember you by.
Perhaps that is why I have not
washed it away.

Morning

You offered two arms
and a hovering warmth.
It cast it's shadows through my window.
Venetian blinds break the angels apart
until it's all too real.
You clearly gave me night.
You simply left me morning.

What I Am

Checkered dress,
nose on the sliding glass door
begging for you to let me in
begging for you to touch me
time creates a blur
I am not that girl anymore

Looking up at you,
for approval, for love, for a snowman
feet wet with frost, eyelids of ice
praying you'll stop this pain
praying you won't hurt me
interpretations delete the words

Dancing a dance, that you wanted
a character to handle your baggage;
give you a new ticket, take you
anywhere you want to go - so that,
I don't have to be here.
Time freezes the globe

I used to look up to you,
eating your compliments because they
filled the spaces; needing your skin
to make myself real.
I am no longer invisible.
I am not that girl anymore.

Time has made me solid,
I believe time has killed you.

And you are moving again
with your own demons
and I know to look away.
I know your eyes hold nothing
but a reflection of my own loss.

I'm not a girl needing you anymore.
I'm not a little girl.

If There Ever Was A Reason

I'm trying not to do those crazy things.
I'm trying not to cry when I explode.
I'm trying anything to be someone other
than the woman who loves you.

You have said you do not think of me that way
but I remember lying beneath your brown eyes,
your face glistening with sweat ---
I think you thought of me differently then.

You want to say you have given me something,
that perhaps you freed me from those demons
that raped me in the closet,
that perhaps you showed me something else,
polished and beautiful
and begging for our touch.
But that is a justification for yourself, only.

Please understand
that I need you to show me I could be loved
that I warrant soft touch and sweet ecstasy
that I'm worth the risk to believe in.

No. I would not have chosen this,
I wouldn't throw it away so easy.
I want to run to you right now,
take your face in my hands
and dance against your flesh
until you cannot turn away.
I'd like to think there is enough of a reason
to explore this glory. To take the silent vow
of an occasional dance. Of a trip to that place
where you let me live.

And it is not fair of me, I know
to ask you to shoulder half my demons,
to redeem the sins of horrid men you never knew

but if there was ever a reason
to bend the rules, to take that risk,
please let it be me.

Please hold me again
inside that land where I saw a different woman
one other than this girl with fearful
trembling hands, clutching this pen,
grasping for words
to erase her world.

Letting Go

I stand in yesterday's bath water
seeing only a crescent moon of you

you throw the stars down to me

I cannot catch them
I recoil like a lost country

I let you go.

Has anyone ever told you
you look a little like Antarctica?
With your cold words

I stand in the remnants of a little girl's hope chest praying for
your wings to break

for you to fall

Vagabond

It is this newness that we love,
the vagueness of each other's skin-
ignoring that the morning shall take that too.

We believe in words never owned by us,
tracing the questions on each other's bodies
while our mouths immerse for answers,
seeking refuge from the world's haunts.

I know I am too far gone
to know my own soul.
And you confess the same,
as if that might lead us
back to a nonexistent dawn.

Words fade from your lips
as if you have them all to spare
as if they were your creation,
an ally to conquer one's soul.
Language spoken as if night
might change it's meaning.
You expect me to let dawn's
wash of color, make me forget.

continued

To lead me to a place where I do not question
how daylight changes words' meaning.

In that moment between dawn and waking
I remember still -
The dampness of your skin on mine,
the words you whispered inside a night
that only I believed in.

Yet, I know I am your God.
You whispered that in my ear
as our bodies thrashed to hold
a night that was already gone.

And you think you have left no trace
that you remembered to take all with you.
But in that moment where we crossed that line
you forgot I was a poet.

You have left me my poems.

In closing...

This collection was completed during the summer months of 1997. In October of 1997, I lost someone very dear to me. This last poem is for him...

October

I stand within this room
blanked and stripped of your essence,
wishing you might turn around
call my name
say it's a joke
praying for something
to take it all back
to rewind to yesterday
when you were still here.

You walked on water,
we dreamt inside stars
trading childhood dreams
and day into night—
you held my hand
and now I hold yours.
Searching for a way
to erase what I witness
to erase what I see.

And inside October's fall light
you let go
while all of us

try so desperately
to hang on.

Brushing your pictures with
hands that once held yours.
Rock - paper - scissors -
learning to snap...
those days we were too young
to realize how we had so little
while having it all

There are no words
to frame your soul
to capture this gold
as we helplessly watch
these days slip away
searching for your face, a sign
a world still with you.

I want to revisit the past.
Take you back, take me back,
replay the scene a bit differently.

continued

We look for reasons in forests
where none exist.
We look for answers
while eagles drift by.

Only questions rest on wings.

And though I can't understand
what has happened here—
I tuck our pictures
between your palms.

You have always held me
and I want you to still.
my brother, my father, my friend
I know you will

I know you will.

A portion of the profits from the sale of this book will be donated to the Caleb Feiereisen memorial fund.

Acknowledgments

My heartfelt thanks...

to Art, for all your kind words and phone calls throughout both my life and writing career. To Don Arenz (wherever you are) for your belief in both me and my abilities. To Sheree Anderson for all those cold, North Dakota, walks to Kinkos during college. To Greg A. for too many reasons to list. To Robynn, who I shared my first poems with- thanks for listening and asking for more. To Scott & Jill for always being there. And to my Mother, thank you for your constant support and encouragement through all of my trials and triumphs.

ABOUT THE AUTHOR

Brook Noel has been writing poetry since the age of six. Her poems have appeared in literary magazines throughout the United States, Canada and Europe. Raised in northern Wisconsin, Noel summers at her childhood home and spends the rest of the year in Portland.

EDUCATIONAL AND GROUP DISCOUNTS ARE AVAILABLE FOR
MORE INFORMATION WRITE TO CHAMPION PRESS, LTD.

Please photocopy this page to order additional copies of *Shadows Of A Vagabond*. Or order on-line at our web site, www.championpress.com.

QUANTITY

_____ *Shadows Of A Vagabond*, by Brook Noel. $12 softcover. Plus $2.95 shipping and handling for one copy, $1 more for each additional copy

_____ Payment enclosed
_____ Please charge my ___ Visa ___ MasterCard

Account Number _____

Expiration Date _____

Signature _____

Name as it appears on card _____

Name _____

Address _____

City _____ State _____ Zip _____

Day Phone _____

Autograph Copy Yes No Personalize to: _____

MAIL FORM TO:

Champion Press, Ltd.

264 S. LaCienega Blvd., Suite 1064

Beverly Hills, CA 90211

The author maintains a mailing list for new releases, news and tour appearances. A list is also maintained by Champion Press, Ltd.

To be added to the author's personal mailing list and/or the list maintained by Champion Press, Ltd., visit our web site at

www.championpress.com

or send your request to:

Champion Press, Ltd.

264 S. LaCienega Blvd., Suite 1064

Beverly Hills, CA 90211